Letters to

My Mother

BY:

Apostle Vincent J. Gilchrist

Published by
Eagles Word Christian Publisher
New York

I LOVE YOU, MOMMIE.

LETTERS WRITTEN TO MY VERY MAGNIFICENT MOTHER.

BY APOSTLE VINCENT J. GILCHRIST

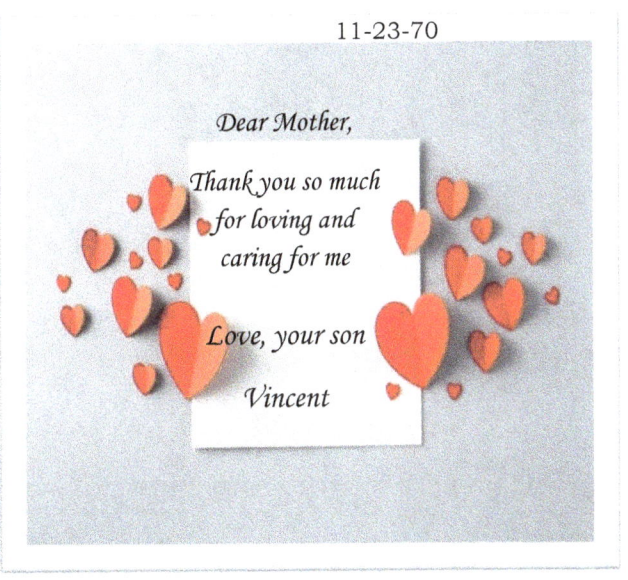

11-23-70

Dear Mother,

Thank you so much for loving and caring for me

Love, your son

Vincent

Psalm 34:8 (AMP)

O taste and see that the Lord [our God] is good!

Contents

Special Dedication

This book is affectionately dedicated to the loving memory of my dear, precious, loving mother, Mary Elizabeth (Sunshine) Gilchrist, who was the matriarch of my family. I thank you for being the example of love, strength, and integrity.

Your love gave my life purpose and direction. Mommy, your life was such a genuine example of the fruit of the spirit: love, joy, peace, patience, kindness, goodness, faithfulness, gentleness, and self-control.

You taught me many magnificent things; among them was how to laugh and smile, but most importantly, to love. The memories of my upbringing in your house have had a profound impact on my life.

You were the precious jewel that God had given to me, and I truly thank Him for allowing your life to impact my life in such a positive way.

You were my greatest cheerleader, and because of that I can say that yes, I WILL make it! Knowing how much you loved me and how proud you were of me was the driving force that helped me to develop into the unique and magnificent person that I am today.

You kept me in church starting at the young age of four, and you did not compromise the Word of God for anyone (you taught me to do the same). As a result, here I stand today as a witness to the scripture *"point your kids in the right direction – when they're old they won't be lost."* *(Proverbs 22:6, MSG)*

What an honor it was to have been not only loved by you, but also adopted and raised by you. It was my blessing to have you in my life. I will forever cherish your memory and I will never forget you! Until that great day when I see you again, I will be missing you.

Dedications

To the late Bishop Edward Lee Chamble, the late Bishop F. D. Washington, the late Pastor Timothy Wright

I thank you all for your great leadership and all that you have taught me. I miss you all so very much.

———————

To my two brothers (the late Deacon Lacy Littles, and the late George W. Littles)

You both continually encouraged me to excel in all that I do, and to always put my best foot forward.

———————

To my friend, the late Bishop Willie Frankie Jones, Jr.

I thank you for being a true friend and a positive force; always helping and encouraging me. I miss you.

To the late Pastor Gloria E. Knight and the late Pastor Patricia D.B. Burrows

Thank you for your love and encouragement.

To the late Elder Robert L. Taylor, Sr. You were indeed an encouragement, and blessing to me.

To my cousin (the late Mary A. Machen) whom I affectionately, and appreciatively called "Aunt Mary"

Thank you very much for loving me and caring for me. I love and miss you.

In Memoriam

In loving memory of those who are now departed.

Revelation 14:13 (MSG)

I heard a voice out of Heaven, "Write this: Blessed are those who die in the Master from now on; how blessed to die that way!" "Yes," says the Spirit, "and blessed rest from their hard, hard work. None of what they've done is wasted: God blesses them for it all in the end."

Acknowledgements

First, I would like to thank my Lord and Savior Jesus Christ for His many blessings. Without Him, my life would be nothing, and nothing that is happening now would be possible.

I want to thank my wonderful family for loving and caring for me.

I want to give thanks to my magnificent Pastor and Godfather, Apostle Levar A. Williams, and his wife Evangelist Jeanett Williams. Thank you for your leadership and all the love that you have showered upon me. Continue to preach God's Holy Word.

Special thanks to my marvelous God-mother, Mother Alice Goodson. I want you to know that I cherish you. Thank you for taking the time to encourage me. I love and appreciate you so very much.

To my spiritual sister and prayer partner (Prophetess, Missionary Gloria J. Byer), Thank you for the many times you have answered my numerous phone calls just to pray for me, but then we ended up having phone church! Thank you for your love, support, and time that you have taken to keep me encouraged. I not only thank you, but I thank God for you.

How Wonderful

By Apostle Vincent J. Gilchrist

How wonderful it is to be able to take the time to write what you feel to a special someone that you love. These letters that I have written express my true thoughts, love, and appreciation for my mother. Some were written when I was a little boy. The one that I wrote on the day of my adoption in February 1983, is one of my favorites; others were written as I was growing into adulthood.

Anyone who knows me well enough knows that I save everything! Especially anything having to do with my mother. I could not believe that I had saved all the letters that I had written over the years – but I am glad that I did so.

My love for my mother was deeper than words alone could express. I miss her so much! It has been thirty-two years, but I still mourn her passing like it was yesterday. I miss her big, lovely, warm smile, and her hugs. But in all that mourning, I still rejoice because I know that I will see her again. I believe that with all my heart and soul. I gratefully give thanks to the Lord for all the special times that we shared, and I look forward to that eternity with her and the Lord who loves us and created us all.

Mother, you stood by me, always loyal and faithful. You believed the best about me and gave me wings to soar. Because of you, I believed that I could do anything. Many times, you were my source of strength when I was weak, and my eyes when I could not see.

You taught me to believe in God for myself, and to lean on Him as personal Lord and Savior, healer, deliverer, provider, protector, comforter, father, friend and soon-coming King. It was you that nurtured the seeds of faith in my life.

You taught me to never give up or lose faith. Your astounding wisdom and guidance safely navigated me through much of my life, and your abundant grace and open arms, helped me to hold my head up when I did not always get things quite right.

Through you I first experienced unselfish, forgiving, and enduring love – the kind that outlasts the test of time...the kind that never fails. I also learned to be responsible, polite, respectful, and courteous to others. You also taught me to stand up for myself when necessary, and to stand firm in what I believe. You always encouraged me to reach for the stars and work hard toward my goals.

Most of all, I thank God for giving you as such a great example for me to follow and giving me the opportunity to know and accept Jesus Christ for myself. You played an active role in my life, especially where my relationship with God was concerned. You impressed upon me to develop a habit of maintaining and grooming my relationship with God, by not just constantly reading the Word to me, but also explaining it as well.

I thank you mother, and every day of my life I appreciate you still. I love you mother!

Mother I learned that I could do all things through Christ that gives me strength. All things work out for good for them that love the Lord. And, in all I have learned to give thanks. Without some rain in my life, I am sure that I would not have learned to appreciate the sunshine that I do have in my life. I have discovered time and time again that with each passing day, and with every hello and goodbye, there is a new lesson that I have gained.

Romans 10:13 (NIV)

"Everyone who calls on the name of the Lord will be saved."

Psalm 34:1 (KJV)

I will bless the Lord at all times: His praise shall continually be in my mouth.

Psalm 13:5-6 (AMPC)

But I have trusted, leaned on, and been confident in your mercy and loving-kindness; my heart shall rejoice and be in high spirits in Your salvation.

I will sing to the Lord because He has dealt bountifully with me.

Psalm 103:2

Bless (affectionately, gratefully praise) the Lord, O my soul, and forget not [one of] all His benefits.

July 25, 1969

Dear Mommie,

I want to thank you for the delicious food that you cooked for my third birthday. You are the greatest!

Love your son,
Vincent

November 23, 1970 (Thursday)

Dear Mama,

You are the only one that deeply holds a special place in my heart. I thank God that He blessed you to be my mother, and I want you to know that you are the greatest mother in the world!

You have greatly enriched my life and made the world a much better place for me to live. For this I owe you my sincerest thanks. Thank you, thank you, thank you.

Most of all, I thank the Almighty God for He is so good to me, and He has blessed me in so many ways and there are not enough words to tell it all.

Dear Mama,

I just want you to know how glad I am that you led me to the Lord and how glad I am that I truly gave my life to Him.

I want you to know that I am so happy that the Lord is in my life and Jesus truly brought the sunshine in my life. I thank God.

Love your son,
Vincent

This letter was written when I was a four-year-old little boy.

Thanksgiving night at 11:00 PM

I want to thank you for a very delicious Thanksgiving dinner that you have magnificently cooked.

This letter was written when I was four years old.

January 13, 1976

Dear Ma,

I love and thank you for everything that you have done for me. Thank you for your good cooking and I really enjoyed all my food.

Love your son,
Vincent

Dear Mama,

I want to thank you for teaching me how to cook my first meal tonight. You taught me how to make macaroni and cheese, mixed vegetables, and fried chicken. This was the best birthday dinner I have ever had; it was delicious, and I enjoyed all the food that I cooked for my tenth birthday. Once again, I thank you very much, and I love you so much!

Love your son,
Vincent

Dear Mommy,

I want you to know that February 18, 1983, is quickly approaching. This is the day that I will officially become your son. I cannot wait until that day comes.

Love,
Vincent

Dear Ma,

I want you to know that I am so happy, and I was filled with so much joy as I watched the judge sign the final papers. Now it is official, and I am legally your son! This is so wonderful to me.

James 1:17 (KJV) says "Every good gift and every perfect gift is from above…," so I thank God - the gift He has given me is a wonderful mother. God has answered my prayers, and He is good to me all the time.

I hope I will be as good a son to you as you are a good mother to me. Let me say "thank you" for adopting me and loving and caring for me. I love you very much, and I hope God richly blesses you and keeps you in His loving care.

Love your son,
Vincent

Dear Mom,

I want you to know that I love you, I love you, I love you!

Love you son,
Vincent

Dear Mother,

I want to say Happy Birthday to you, and I hope that you enjoy your special day. Thank you very much for letting me celebrate my fifteenth birthday with you; I enjoyed myself a lot. May God continue to bless you.

Love your son,
Vincent

I want to thank you and my sister Clara for leading me to the Lord. As a result of your praying for me, I received Him into my life. Again, thank you and may God bless you.

Lovingly your son,
Vincent

Dearest Mother,

I just want to let you know that to be adopted by you was one of the greatest gifts that I have ever gotten in my life. One way that God has tremendously blessed me is by giving you to me, and I am thankful to Him for being in your life.

You have brought joy, love, and happiness into my life and I have grown to love you with a special love. That day when you adopted me, I was so happy to know that there was somebody in this world who really and truly loved, and cared for me, when nobody else could or would. You only wanted what was best for me.

I realize that who I am today is due to your good work, and I am glad that you instilled such great discipline and morals in me when I was a child. I did not realize how much of a sacrifice you made then, but now that I have grown up, I appreciate that and all the wonderful things that you have done for me.

I remember as a child, you would say repeatedly to me that "if I do not adopt you, who will"? I must say that I am so glad that you did.

Mother,

I thank you for being strict with me because when you spoke, I learned to obey, because I knew that if I did not, you would have no problem with giving me a good old-fashioned spanking. Mama, you would spank me, and quote scripture at that same time! "Foolishness resides in the heart of a child, but the rod of correction will drive it out." (Prov. 22:15). This was one of your favorite verses. Thank you for never giving up on me.

Proverbs 23:13-14 (MSG)

Don't be afraid to correct your young ones; a spanking won't kill them.

A good spanking, in fact, might save them from something worse than death

.

To love and care for me was a special responsibility, and you did it out of love for me. I do believe with all my heart that you took your mothering seriously. Taking care of the children. you love is incredibly special; God gave you that special love, to love me unconditionally and you did a masterful job in taking care of me. When I look back over my life and remember all the things that you have done for me, and how you devoted yourself to me, I am grateful. You worked extremely hard and made endless sacrifices to raise me.

You taught me to hold my head high and appreciate that God made me for a special purpose. I MUST thank you for disciplining me in the manner that you did. Mama let me say to you that it did work out to be the best for me.

I thank you for the many punishments I got from you because they had a lasting impression on me. I understand that it was your wonderful way of reminding me that there was a wrong way of doing things, and then there was "mama's way" of doing things. You were a tough mother, but I thank you for that. When you said no, you meant NO.

Let me just say that I truly thank you mother, your discipline was the best thing that you could have done for me. Proverbs 23:14 says "Thou shalt beat him with the rod, and shalt deliver his soul from hell." (KJV).

Of course, your way was always the right way. I never doubted your love for me, even when you chastised me, you did it out of love. I just want to say that I absolutely appreciate all of it, because it made me into the person that I am today.

Mother, I miss you more and more with each passing day. I want you to know that you are still loved very much and thought of often. There are many times that I sit and think about you; you will always hold that special place in my heart.

I remember the joy, and the happy times that we had together. Mother, growing up with you was truly a blessing from God above. Such sweet memories, and the smile on your face is a treasure that will last forever. Your comforting words were like music to my ears.

I am so glad that you taught me to only trust in God and rely on Him when things got hard. Now I can say that your legacy lives deep within me and will never fade away. I miss you and will forever love you.

Lovingly yours, your son,
Elder Vincent J. Gilchrist

Dear Mother,

I thank God for allowing you to adopt me when you did – before someone else did. I shudder to think of how my life would have otherwise turned out. I remember at the age of three-years-old, I came to you and told you that I wanted to be a preacher one day, and you said to me "you can be anything you want to be if you put your mind to it." And today mother, I am a great minister of the Lord Jesus Christ. I thank you for encouraging me when I was a child (it meant so much to me). Thank you, mother. I love you and still miss you dearly.

Love your son,
Elder Vincent J. Gilchrist

June 13, 2007 (Wednesday)

Dear Mother,

Thank you for always praying for me, and with me. I want you to know that some of the happiest memories from my childhood include you teaching me how to pray and showing me how important prayer is. You taught me to pray before eating my dinner, before going to bed, and first thing in the morning. I thank you from the bottom of my heart. I love and miss you.

Love you son,
Vincent

Dear Mama,

As I write you this letter, I find myself missing you terribly. The memories of you live on forever in my heart. I would like to think that God gave special attention to the memory cells in my brain when He fearfully and wonderfully created me.

Mama, you genuinely taught me how to pray, and I thank you more and more each day for doing that. As far back as I can remember, you required that every night we prayed as a family. I may not have liked it then, but I am so glad now. I love to pray, and just as I was taught as a child, I get down on my knees. I want to tell you mother, that I thank you for those special times that we prayed together. I love you dearly.

Love your son,
Elder Vincent J. Gilchrist

Dear Mama,

I want you to know that even though you are no longer here, you are always with me, and your love still surrounds me. You have always been special to me; your smile brightened up my day! You touched my life in a way that no one else could and made it complete. Words cannot express all that having you in my life meant to me, and when I am feeling sad, I think of you. I will never forget you mama.

Love your son,
Elder Vincent J. Gilchrist

July 8, 2007 (Sunday)

Dear Mama,

Thank you for taking the time to counsel and encourage me, it meant a great deal to me. I remember you saying to me, many times, that you were glad to be my mother. Thank you for loving me so much.

Mama, you have greatly affected my life. You helped me to understand the importance of knowing my life's purpose and exercising my faith. I am so glad that you would always tell me to "pray about it, wait on the Lord for an answer, then DO IT — step out in faith and God will lead you!" Well, mama, I did it! As usual, you were right; thank you. I miss you.

Love your son,
Elder Vincent J. Gilchrist

Dear Mother,

I must say Mother, that you truly were a remarkable mother to me. From the bottom of my heart, I am very thankful that you taught me to believe. You taught me to believe in God before anything else, and to believe in myself.

I saw how you valued God's Word in your own life – feeding the habit of personal prayer and looking to Him for strength with raising me. You did not seek that strength, wisdom, or comfort in other people, money, position, profession, education, or in any life circumstance.

You understood that people and situations change. Other human beings can immensely affect my life, and you made sure to make me aware that people will and do change. People are up one moment and down the next; they can like you one minute and hate you the next. They may tell you one thing on Monday, but by Sunday they might change their minds. This is not the case with God. These life lessons that you lovingly taught me, I appreciate.

You taught me that God does not change, and He can be counted on. And I will always remember that. Hebrews 13:8 says, "Jesus Christ is the same yesterday and today and forever." Thank you, Mother, for the life lessons that you took the time to teach me. They will be with me for the rest of my life. So, I say again to you Mother, THANK YOU.

Love your son,
Elder Vincent J. Gilchrist

I wrote this letter on my thirty-second birthday.

Dear Mama,

I want to say that you were beautiful and precious to me — my champion and cheerleader. You were an incredibly strong and courageous woman, who always nurtured the gifts and talents in my life.

You were gracious, elegant, smart, intelligent and have always been the quintessential "special lady" in my life. Without a doubt, you were the sweetest person that I knew, and I love you dearly. You are the most cherished delicate flower.

Love,
Elder Vincent J. Gilchrist

I called my mother "Mrs. more precious than rubies." She was a true Proverbs 31:26 woman of God – "She opened her mouth with wisdom and in her tongue was the law of kindness." (KJV). What a magnificent mother that God had given to me!

Proverbs 31:10 (AMPC)

A capable, intelligent, and virtuous woman – who is he who can find her? She is far more precious than jewels *and* her value is far above rubies *or* pearls.

The best things that a mother can do for her child is to teach and lead that child to the Lord. Mama, I want you to know that giving my life to Him was the best decision that I have ever made for myself. As the song says, "I've decided to make Jesus my choice," and He has done so many great and wonderful things for me.

Dear Reader,

This magnificent book was written from my heart to encourage you. Within the pages are seventeen very touching, encouraging, and special letters that I have benevolently written to my dear and loving mother, who was special and important to me and whom I loved with all my heart.

I want to share these special letters with you and implore you that if you have a mother still in the land of the living, let her know how much she means to you while you have the opportunity to do so.

I pray that this book touches your heart and that you enjoy reading it as much as I have enjoyed writing it.

Apostle Vincent J. Gilchrist

About Vincent Gilchrist

Apostle Vincent J. Gilchrist is a native of Brooklyn N.Y. He is an anointed preacher, gospel singer, song writer, and author. His desire is to ensure that men, women, and children come to know Jesus as their Savior.

www.ingramcontent.com/pod-product-compliance
Lightning Source LLC
Chambersburg PA
CBHW070355130626
46556CB00007B/3176